Simple Truths

A Journaling Devotional for Teen Girls

Therin Jones Fenner

Dedication

To every young woman who has
prayed for her faith to become real
and color all she does.

Introduction

Welcome to *Simple Truths*.

Not everything is true, and not every truth is simple—but here, at the intersection of both, this little book stakes its claim. God's love for you—and the implications that love has for your life—doesn't have to be that complicated.

Please believe me when I tell you: you are an amazing piece of God's creation. You are *fearfully* and *wonderfully* made. You are God's beloved daughter, and He has *plans* for you. You can rest in that. You can be assured.

Life seems to move pretty quickly. Sometimes, we leave ourselves so little margin around our commitments—school, sports, work, friends—that we barely have time to take a breath, let alone feed our souls. *But your soul needs nourishment.* God loves you no matter what, but one of the most amazing things you can do for yourself is *feel* that love daily and grow in awareness of it. God's love for you is deep and broad, and it lasts forever—and knowing that can change *everything*. Even when things get complicated, when you experience or encounter brokenness and pain, the simple truth of God's love and care is there with you.

That's where this devotional comes in.

How to Use this Book

What you hold in your hands is a 52-week journey for your soul. We as Christians believe that God speaks to us through His Holy word. It's been around for a while, but it doesn't rust, wither, or decay—it is the Eternal Truth of God's redemptive action. One of my favorite things about the Bible is that it's so rich, we can't read and digest it like novels of a favorite series. We have to engage it again and again, always seeking new understanding, new insights. It's written for lifelong relationship.

Over these next 52 weeks, you'll reflect on a short piece of scripture each week. I invite you to re-read the scripture and the reflection each day of the week if you're able. At the end of the reflection for the week, there will be a prompt for engaging—something to consider, a new spiritual practice to try, or an action to take in your life. (Some of them may stump you for a little bit but keep trying; the biggest questions can have the largest impacts on our lives.) There's also a place for you to record your thoughts on the scripture for the week. Imagine what a wonderful record you'll have of your journey by the end of the year! May it reflect the richness and depth of your ongoing relationship with Christ.

The weeks (and readings) are divided into three sections, to reflect the simple truth of our faith: *You are wonderfully made... to love God... and to love your neighbor as yourself.*

So, that's it! Read, reflect, and record. This is for *you*.

A note on the biblical translation used

For this devotional, I've used the New Revised Standard Vision (NRSV) of the biblical text. There are, of course, other translations. Reading more than one reputable translation can "open up" the text for you in new ways. Sometimes, a single word change can help us to hear God in a new way. Feel free to do an internet search for other translations like The Message or New King James Version to give new dimension to a verse you're reflecting on for the week.

OK, I think that's all the housekeeping. Let's go!

Part One:

You are wonderfully made

Week One: __/__/__
From Nothing Came Everything

In the beginning God created the heaven and the earth. And the earth was without form, and void; and darkness was upon the face of the deep. And the Spirit of God moved upon the face of the waters. And God said, Let there be light: and there was light. – Genesis 1:1-3

Out of nothing, God created everything. Can you even imagine what a "formless void" looks like? It's a hard thing to picture. In the beginning, there was *nothing*. From that nothingness, God created all that we see around us—the sky above us, the earth beneath us, and the plants and creatures all around us. Literally *everything* was crafted and set into motion by a loving, imaginative Creator.

We're reminded in a real way of God's creativity when we glance up at a watercolor sunset or feel the warmth of the sun on our backs. If you were to kneel beside a flower and study it, you'd get an even more concrete sense of the intricate order of God's design. Sometimes, people experience special closeness to God when they survey the vastness of God's creation from, say, a mountaintop—some people call these "mountaintop experiences." There's something about the world around us that naturally inspires awe, reverence.

Do you experience the same wonder when you catch your own reflection in the mirror? You should. Scripture tells us that God knitted you together in your mother's womb; you, too, are a result of God's creativity and imagination. Just as we would deeply know something we sculpted—the places we had to draw the clay a little thin, or where we left a small, partial thumbprint—God knows every inch of us. We are part of God's living artwork. We're works in progress, to be sure, but we are intimately known and loved the way only a Creator could know and love us.

engage

Consider: Does it make you think of yourself differently when you remind yourself that you're a piece of God's wonderful creation?

Week Two: __/__/__
The Greatest Story Ever Told

In the beginning was the Word, and the Word was with God, and the Word was God. He was in the beginning with God. All things came into being through him, and without him not one thing came into being. What has come into being in him was life and the life was the light of all people. The light shines in the darkness, and the darkness did not overcome it. – John 1:1-5

In the prologue from the Gospel of John, we hear the story of creation in a new way. At the beginning, it wasn't just God the Creator; the "Word," another way of talking about the Son of God, or Christ, was also present. Through him, life enters the world—both the divine life of creation and the eternal life Jesus brings to those who accept him. This life was the light of all people; a light that the darkness, no matter how widespread or how scary, cannot overcome or extinguish. That should give you incredible, persistent hope—the kind of hope that, itself, is a light in the darkness. The life begun in creation, the life born as a baby in Jesus Christ, represents something eternal that no worldly evil can put out.

Of all four gospels, John may have the most "cosmic" perspective; he starts with the biggest lens possible: the creation of the universe. God the Father, the Son, and the Holy Spirit are all present, playing vital roles. We get an even stronger sense that each of us is part of a story that goes all the way back to the beginning of time. Think of the longest novel you've ever read, and then multiply that by a thousand—that should give you a sense of the length and complexity of God's story.

In other words, YOU are a character in a story that began billions of years ago, out of the "formless void" we learned about in Genesis. God's story is so rich and so full, with so many characters, every one of whom was specially written by God—and the story is still unfolding *right now*.

engage

Go for it: Every story of faith is completely original. How would you tell yours? Choose someone in your life—either a close friend or someone you're just getting to know—and try telling them the story of your faith. (If you'd rather just write it down, that's okay, too! The point is: Your story is an incredible and important part of God's story.)

Week Three: __/__/__
An Earth Full of God's Creatures

O Lord, how manifold are your works! In wisdom you have made them all; the earth is full of your creatures. – Psalm 104:24

Some people call the Psalms the "prayer book of the Bible." If you're ever looking for the words to say to God—whether you're going through a challenging time or not—there will be a Psalm that you can pray. The Psalms give us words when we can't find them ourselves.

Many of the Psalms have praise for God, who created us—and everything around us! "The earth is full of your creatures," the Psalmist writes. Your dog? A creature of God. Your brother? A child of God. The beetle you saw scamper across the cabin floor at overnight camp? Also created by God. Not all creatures were made in God's image the way humankind was, but all were lovingly created just the same. Each piece of God's creation, no matter how tiny, shows us how creative and whimsical God is. Did you know an iguana can hold its breath for up to 28 minutes underwater? Or that dolphins and some other animals can sleep with just one half of their brains at a time? Or even that a giraffe can clean its ears with its tongue? Animals can adapt to their environments in incredible ways, and all of them are masterpieces-within-the-masterpiece of God's creation.

This week try to look at the world around you with new eyes—ready to see how incredible the created world is. Every leaf, every flower, every classmate, every bird—a masterpiece.

engage

Practice: Pick a psalm to pray this week. Try praying it a few times, or maybe even every day. How did it feel? Did it give you words for something you've been feeling?

Week Four: __/__/__
Stewards of the Earth

So God created humankind in his image, in the image of God he created them; male and female he created them. God blessed them, and God said to them, 'Be fruitful and multiply, and fill the earth and subdue it; and have dominion over the fish of the sea and the birds of the air and over every living thing that moves upon the earth.' - Genesis 1:27-28.

People have written whole books about the meaning of a single word in this passage—"dominion." What do you think it means to have dominion over every living thing that moves upon the earth? Do you think it means that we are meant to use all of God's creation for our own purpose—however we like? Or do you think it means we, as the beings made in God's image, are responsible for safeguarding the rest of God's creation?

We may think of rulers when hear the word "dominion" now—but in the biblical context, the likeliest metaphor was sheep tending. A shepherd had "dominion" over the sheep because he was meant to protect and care for them from a place of competence.

The word sometimes used for this idea is "stewardship." We are meant to be "stewards" of God's good creation, not using it for our own gratification in the short term but protecting it for the long term, for the common *good*. We're meant to take *care* of it for the next generation. Imagine receiving an indoor bonsai plant as a gift. You'd find someplace to set it, maybe a windowsill, where it could receive the right amount of sunlight. You might mist it with warm water every morning. At intervals, you'd have to do more serious work—cutting away part of the roots and trimming the branches, for example. If you do your job well, your bonsai might outlive you! We obviously can't exercise this level of care for every plant and animal in the world—but we can live our lives in a way that shows the welfare of plants and animals matters. All of creation is a masterful web—and we're not just tenders of it; we're a *part* of that web.

engage

Consider: What does stewardship mean to you? How do you practice Christian stewardship in your daily life?

Week Five: __/__/__
The World as a Classroom

The heavens are telling the glory of God;
And the firmament proclaims his handiwork.
Day to day pours forth speech,
And night to night declares knowledge.
There is no speech, nor are there words;
Their voice is not heard;
Yet their voice goes out through all the earth,
And their words to the end of the world. – Psalm 19:1-4a

How does God speak to you? For the Psalmist, knowledge of God is passed on through God's creation itself; even without saying a word, God speaks with a voice that "goes out through all the earth" and "to the end of the world." Those "mountaintop experiences" we were talking about a few weeks ago—that's a way of God reaching out to us and reaching *into* us.

Of course, God speaks to each of us in different ways. We're made to hear His voice, made to know Him and be loved by Him, but we're also each of us made differently. For some of us, getting lost in scripture or prayer is how we feel the love God has for us, His Creation. For others, the warmth of a healthy human relationship is a way we experience a glimmer of the beauty and goodness of God. Or maybe you experience God most fully when you're surrounded by nature, stunned silly by how exquisite God's creation is.

The Psalmist may have fallen into that last category. He sees the wonder of God "on tour" in the sky and "on exhibit" on the horizon. The earth is a classroom where he learns about *who God is* through *what God has created*. It's a learning that happens without speech. The Truth that is proclaimed night and day, to the ends of the earth, is one that goes beyond words.

engage

Go for it: Watch a sunset this week. Say a prayer as watercolor-reds fill the sky. What does God's creation teach you about who God is?

Week Six: __/__/__
Fearfully and Wonderfully Made

For it was you who formed my inward parts;
You knit me together in my mother's womb.
I praise you, for I am fearfully and
Wonderfully made.
Wonderful are your works;
That I know very well. – Psalm 139:13-14

Can you pray the words of this psalm? Are they words you believe, to the core of your being? Sometimes, there's so much coming at us from so many different directions, we have trouble appreciating how amazing it is that we are here at all—that we are flesh and bone and heart and imagination. You may already be the size of an adult now—but once, you were smaller than a baseball. You had translucent skin, fragile bones, and a heartbeat that made your whole body pulse. God has followed you the whole way. He has watched your greatest achievements and walked beside you through your biggest disappointments. He knows you inside and out, and He loves you exactly as you are. If God, the Creator of this vast universe, considers you a work of art, shouldn't you like yourself, too?

When I was 16, I had such terrible acne that I thought it was all anyone ever saw when they looked at me. It made me incredibly self-conscious. A lot of my self-worth got wrapped up in my complexion—and all I wanted, all I prayed for, was this acne to disappear overnight. Though it did eventually become much more manageable, I reflect on that time now with bewilderment. Why did I let something so superficial affect me at my roots? Why couldn't I see myself as God saw me—a precious being He had loved since before I *had* a consciousness? I praise God for the awareness that I am fearfully and wonderfully made—a dynamic work of art.

engage

Consider: Is there a part of you that you have trouble accepting or embracing? What's holding you back? Do you think God sees you the way you see yourself—and which is the truth?

Week Seven: __/__/__
You are Enough

For we are what he has made us, created in Christ Jesus for good works, which God prepared beforehand to be our way of life. – *Ephesians 2:10*

The experience of not feeling good enough is nearly universal. All of us, at some point in time or in some circumstance, feel like we're not "good enough." We're not pretty enough, maybe, for our crush. Not smart enough for the college we want to attend. Not funny enough for our friends. Feeling like "not enough" is common—but it's a lie.

You. Are. Enough. You are God's amazing, beloved daughter. That isn't a joke or a fantasy; that's the truest truth I can share with you. God knows you and loves you, just as you are. God doesn't compare you with anyone else; you are the only YOU there is.

And—it gets better—God has plans for you. Wonderful, exhilarating, deeply fulfilling plans for good. We don't always understand the big picture when we're stuck in the weeds, but God's story is about redemption and beauty, and it's a story very much still underway in you and the world around you. You're created to do "good works" in the way of Jesus, and to do those good works in a way that only YOU can. Frederick Buechner, an American pastor and theologian, wrote once that vocation (that is, "calling"—what you're meant to be doing in this world) is "the place where our deep gladness meets the world's deep need." In other words, we are each created to do the good works of Christ in the specific way that resonates deeply with *our* souls. For that, you have everything you need—you are enough.

engage

Consider: Do you feel like you are enough? What—or who—keeps you from feeling that way?

Week Eight: __/__/__
Beloved, from Head to Toe

"Are not five sparrows sold for two pennies? Yet not one of them is forgotten in God's sight! But even the hairs of your head are all counted. Do not be afraid; you are of more value than many sparrows." – Luke 12:6-7

We may pay little attention to the birds outside our window—but God knows all of them. To God, each and every sparrow is a treasured part of God's creation. Imagine, then, how much God cares for you, a young person made in his image, a woman he knows and loves through and through. In God's sight, Jesus assures us, you'll never been unseen or overlooked. God is so familiar with you—every part of your body and soul—that He has numbered the hairs on your head.

Jesus shares this good news with his disciples because he's worried they'll feel bullied by others in the religious community. He's worried that they will regard other *people's* opinions as supremely important—when what really matters is that we are intimately known and accepted by *God.* There will always be people in your life who think you should behave differently, talk differently, look differently. They may even understand God differently and disagree about how to follow God. Sometimes, these other people will have wonderful guidance for us—but Jesus reminds us that God is truly at the center. (After all, Jesus didn't ask us to follow other Christians; he asked us to follow *him.*) Communities of faith are made to encourage us on the journey—and they will come and go—but our relationship with God endures forever.

engage

Consider: Is there someone in your life whose opinion matters too much? A parent? A friend? A crush? Our stock may rise and fall with people in our lives, but God always considers us dear beyond measure. When we're rooted in Him, we can be assured we are valued no matter what we do.

Week Nine: __/__/__
Gifted by the Spirit

Now there are varieties of gifts, but the same Spirit; and there are varieties of services, but the same Lord; and there are varieties of activities, but it is the same God who activates all of them in everyone. To each is given the manifestation of the Spirit for the common good. – 1 Corinthians 12:4-7

We tend to think a lot about which "talents" we have—especially in the years leading up to college applications and job interviews. Spiritual gifts are a little different; spiritual gifts are things with which you've been entrusted—abilities and aptitudes given to you by the Holy Spirit so you can participate in God's kingdom in a particular way.

Scripture identifies at least twenty "spiritual gifts," either mentioned by Paul in his letters or present in the early church. These spiritual gifts, we believe, were given to individual followers of Christ so they might become more *like* Christ—but also so they might help build up the body of Christ. An example of spiritual gift mentioned in scripture is "leadership." In the biblical context, someone with this gift wasn't necessarily assertive or authoritative; she was like a shepherd. Are you good at protecting and caring for others? Another spiritual gift is counseling. Do you give people personal care and attention? Do they tend to trust and confide in you? Anything that helps us share and spread God's love and the good news of His kingdom is a spiritual gift. In fact, that's how we would test something we thought might be a spiritual gift; we'd ask, "Is this an aspect of who I am that helps me serve the common good?"

You may feel stumped when someone asks you, "What's your talent?" We're not all good at the piano. We don't all make wonderful-tasting pies. But all followers of Christ have been given gifts by the Holy Spirit—because we've all been called to play an active role in God's story as it unfolds right now, before our eyes.

engage

Consider: Do you have gifts of the Holy Spirit that you may have been overlooking? How do you use them to spread Christ's love?

Week Ten: __/__/__
Child of God

See what love the Father has given us, that we should be called children of God; and that is what we are. The reason the world does not know us is that it did not know him. Beloved, we are God's children now; what we will be has not yet been revealed. What we do know is this: when he is revealed, we will be like him, for we will see him as he is. – 1 John 3:1-2

You are precious to God! You are a prize beyond compare—irreplaceable, totally known, totally loved. Hopefully, these last few months, as you've been reading that message here in these pages, you've also felt it deeply resonate in your being. Maybe you've even felt God affirm it within you through the work of the Holy Spirit in your life. You are, before anything else, a beloved child of God. All our many, other identities are subordinate or secondary to our identity in Christ.

Of course, this means we are, in some fundamental way, foreigners here on earth. We know in our hearts that we don't belong here; we are subjects of the Kingdom of Heaven, a kingdom that is ordered very differently than this world. In some ways, the Kingdom of Heaven is the mirror image of what we experience in this world—a place where everything is reversed. In the Kingdom of Heaven, the last will be first and the vulnerable and meek will be seen for having true strength. This is what the writer of 1 John means when he says, "the world does not know us." Just as the world did not fully understand the ministry and love of Jesus Christ, it doesn't fully understand those who follow Christ. The world isn't necessarily "opposing us," it just doesn't *get* us because we don't operate the way it does. We see strength in vulnerability, emptiness in worldly possessions, and indiscriminate love as the most powerful force there is. We're not trying to "win" over others but to live into our true, full identity as God's children.

engage

Consider: What "identities" would you claim for yourself? Are you a daughter? A citizen of your country? An athlete? An artist? Where does "Child of God" go on your list?

Part Two:

To love God

Week Eleven: __/__/__
The Most Beautiful Love Story Ever Told

For God so loved the world that he gave his only Son, so that everyone who believes in him may not perish but may have eternal life. — John 3:16

This is the Gospel in a nutshell: God loved the world he created so deeply, so dearly, that he was willing to sacrifice his beloved Son, Jesus Christ, that we might be reconciled to him forever. For many of us, this is too large an act for us to comprehend; we spend a lifetime coming to terms with what God's sacrifice means about God's love.

God loves *you* so deeply, so truly, that he removed every impediment to spending eternity with you. All that is asked is that you *believe* it and place your faith and trust in Him. This is an incredible bargain; we've done nothing to earn or deserve God's love, or God's sacrificial act on the cross, but God sought us out. God pursued us. God knew everything about us—including the ways we seek to suppress, ignore, or shut out his activity in our lives—and He still wanted to be in relationship with us. That's mind-bending.

Jesus' death on the cross that day exposed the world for what it was: a world of violence, captive to a legion of life-choking forces like war, hatred, racism, sexism, consumerism, and greed. The crucified Christ embodied the nonviolent love of God in a world so unequipped to receive that kind of love that it killed the messenger who brought it. Because of that sacrifice, that *compassion*, God opened for us a future of reconciliation—a future where each of us might finally be free—*from* death and *for* an eternity with the loving creator who calls us home.

engage

Practice: Opening our hearts to Christ and believing the truth of his Word isn't an instantaneous event; it's ongoing. This week, pray for deepening belief. As a boy's father cried out before Jesus, "Lord, Help my Unbelief!" This isn't a sign of weakness; it's a sign of growth in your walk with the Lord.

Week Twelve: __/__/__
The Most Radical Love

But God proves his love for us in that while we still were sinners Christ died for us.
— Romans 5:8

You may still be processing the text from last week—but this text from Romans adds a new layer. God reconciled us to him—through Jesus' saving death on the cross—*even though* we did nothing to deserve it. We *still* can't do anything to deserve it. You can follow every commandment, seek to glorify God in all you say and do, and you'll still fall short. You won't be perfect. You'll stumble. You'll doubt God's faithfulness. You'll act out of rage or hurt or fear rather than love. We all do; we're all *human*.

We can't earn what's truly important on our own merits—but God gives everything to us anyway. He gives it to us because He loves us, because He is generous, and because He wants us to be with Him. Without YOU, something is missing, something is incomplete.

Of course, this doesn't mean we shouldn't try to follow the guidance of scripture and the example of Jesus. On some level, we can't help *but* live that way; we've been given the greatest, most amazing gift for free—why wouldn't we respond with joy and gratitude? It does mean, though, that when we fall short of God's example, we're still loved. We're still accepted. We're still a vital member of God's family. That doesn't change.

engage

Practice: Brennan Manning, author of *Ragamuffin Gospel*, writes, "My deepest awareness of myself is that I am deeply loved by Jesus Christ and I have done nothing to earn it or deserve it." This week, try saying out loud to yourself, "I am deeply loved by Jesus Christ." How does it feel? Do you feel silly? Do you believe it? Why?

Week Thirteen: __/__/__
A God Above Everything Else

Hear, O Israel: The LORD is our God, the LORD alone.
— Deuteronomy 6:4

This verse is called the *Shema* (from the Hebrew word for "Hear" at its beginning). Even now, the Shema is at the center of Jewish morning and evening prayer services—encapsulating for the community the totality of God. When the events of the book of Deuteronomy were unfolding, there were many other religions—with many other Gods. The message to God's people was that there is only *one* God—and that's God!

Today, we still encounter people who worship other gods—and I'm not necessarily talking about other religions. Many people, even in the Christian community, place things other than God at the center of their lives. Sometimes, we lose sight of the fact that God is GOD! Nothing else can have the same power or influence in our lives—not friends, family, money, status, or even achievement. We would call these "false idols"—and they crop up all over the place. It's part of our human nature. Those in the Jewish community who recite The Shema daily do so to reorient themselves, to remind themselves over and over again that *God* is at the center and the top—and He can't share that spot with anyone or any *thing* else. With God above everything else we are centered; with God competing with many of other passions, interests, and addictions, we're off-kilter.

engage

Consider: What competes with God for you? Is there something to which you give your time, talent, or heart that gets more of you than God does?

Week Fourteen: __/__/__
No Greater Commandment

One of the scribes came near and heard them disputing with one another, and seeing that he answered them well, he asked him, "Which commandment is the first of all?" Jesus answered, "The first is, 'Hear, O Israel: the Lord our God, the Lord is one; you shall love the Lord your God with all your heart, and with all your soul, and with all your mind, and with all your strength.' The second is this, 'You shall love your neighbor as yourself.' There is no other commandment greater than these."
— Mark 12:28-36

Does some of this scripture sound familiar? It should! When a scribe asked Jesus which commandment is most important, Jesus begins with The Shema. He starts by reorienting us to the idea that there is only one God, above everything else in our lives. We should love Him with our total selves—our heart and soul, our intellect, and our energy.

But that's only part of it—there's another instruction that Jesus feels is worth mentioning, too. The scribe only asked for the first commandment—the "first of all." But Jesus continues: "Love your neighbor as yourself." For Jesus, these were two sides of the same coin. If you love God with your total self, how could you help but love the rest of his creation, including your neighbor?

Later, Jesus tells a story that illustrates just how inclusive "neighbor" is; he doesn't just mean we should love the people who live near us, or think like us. A classmate who follows a different faith from ours, a refugee seeking asylum at our country's border, or a family threatened by conflict on the other side of the world—those are all our neighbors as Christ envisions them. Sometimes, though, our actual neighbors are a great place to start building real relationships where we can offer love and care.

engage

Practice: Do you know your neighbors? Introduce yourself, or just go over to say hello (if you already know them). The first step to the kind of community-building God calls us to is simply knowing *who* is in your community.

Week Fifteen: __/__/__
New Every Morning

This is the day that the Lord has made; let us rejoice and be glad in it.
— Psalm 118:24

In his book *Teach Us to Pray*, Gordon Smith writes that we feel God's love most viscerally, in that deep-in-our-bones kind of way, when we reflect on the blessings in our lives. When we think about the ways we've received more than we've earned, we "get" God's love in a real way. Through gratitude, we get a peek of God's deep "lovingkindness" (*hesed* in Hebrew) for us.

Indeed, when we place our days in perspective, gratitude feels like the *only* response we could offer. We get bogged down in disappointments, small and large, and lose sight of the fact that it's all a gift. Each day when the sun rises anew, and we stretch and get out of our beds, we've been handed another blessing—a chance to love our neighbors better, another day to delight in the beauty of God's creation, an opportunity to grow in love of Him.

I know some women who recite these words from the psalmist every morning when they wake up. One of my friends even has this verse framed by her bedside so it's the first thing she sees when she opens her eyes in the half-light of the morning. It's an orienting verse, a verse that reminds us that God loves us in real, tangible ways, and that the gratitude we feel and express with our lives is the natural response to God's love. God has given you a new day today—what will you do with it?

engage

Practice: If this verse speaks to you, put it next to your bed so you see it every morning when you wake up. Use it to set your intention for the day and remind you that each day of our lives is a precious gift.

Week Sixteen: __/__/__
Jesus is the True Vine

"I am the true vine, and my Father is the vine-grower."
– John 15:1

Of the four Gospels, the book of John stands apart; it frequently gives us a new dimension of the same events in Jesus' life. Here, in John, Jesus is spending the last evening of his earthly life with his disciples. Rather than sharing a meal, the "Last Supper" (as in the other three Gospels), Jesus passes the evening demonstrating how to be a servant—by washing the disciples' feet. With his words and his actions, he is telling them goodbye.

Jesus uses the metaphor of a "vine" here to explain to the disciples what it means to a be connected to him. When we're connected to Christ, like a branch to a vine, we are healthy. We grow and bear fruit. When Christ is in us and we are in Christ (the Bible often uses the word "abide" for this), we are our fullest, most free selves. We love and live as we were meant to; connected to our Creator and given our purpose through Him.

When we become disconnected from Christ, we wither. We move away from God's active presence in the world and feel inwardly the growth of selfishness, ingratitude, fear, and doubt. Even with all our gifts and all our cunning, we can't realize our true potential on our own. We can't reach our true purpose and be the men and women God calls us to be.

engage

Consider: What does it mean for you to feel connected to Christ like a leaf to a vine? Is there a spiritual practice—either one you've tried in this journal or another you'd like to try—that might help you "abide" in Christ?

Week Seventeen: __/__/__
Unstoppable in Christ

I can do all things through Christ who strengthens me.
– Philippians 4:13

Do you remember the verse of the children's song that goes "I am weak, but he is strong?" It's true; we can be pretty weak. We're susceptible to all kinds of sin, and we fall short of God's design for us several times each day. We even fall short of our own best intentions—because we're human beings, not robots.

But in Christ, we have something else. We have the strength of the Living, Loving God—a God who took on our human form as part of a beautiful plan to draw us back into his embrace. Christ endured forty days of temptation by the Devil in the desert; a lifetime of misunderstanding, derision, and persecution; and finally an excruciating death on the cross. There's nothing Christ cannot do.

Through Christ, then, anything is possible. There's nothing beyond our grasp, even in these human forms, because God can truly do the impossible. We can bring this hopefulness, this trust, to all areas of our lives. We might feel God calling us toward a vocation we don't think we'd be "good" at—but God has other plans. We may have given up hope on a relationship with a friend, a family member, or a partner—but sometimes, God can plant amazing new growth in the middle of broken relationships. When you abide in Christ and Christ in you, you put on his otherworldly strength—and nothing in this world can stop what God chooses to do through you.

engage

Practice: Is there a relationship that has been causing you grief? Bring it to God in prayer: *God, I know you're at work in all parts of my life, even the parts that are dark and tangled. I'm so grateful for the renewal that happens only through your Spirit. Please bring that Spirit over my relationship with X. Help us mend wounds, clear up misunderstandings, and demonstrate the love for each other that you modeled for us through your Son. Amen.*

Week Eighteen: __/__/__
We Walk by Trust

Trust in the Lord with all your heart,
and do not rely on your own insight.
In all your ways acknowledge him,
and he will make straight your paths.
— Proverbs 3:5-6

Extra points for those who, last week, lingered over the words *"God chooses to do* through you." Sometimes, some of us think that when we claim Christ as our Lord and Savior, that means we can never be wrong—and anything we choose to do will be blessed by Him. It *is* true (and thank God it is!) that God can redeem even very bad situations. It *isn't* true, though, that love of Christ is something you can use for your own purposes.

As human beings who love Christ, we struggle to always know his will for us. We want a map or even a walkie talkie to clip on our waistbands. Whenever we need God's guidance, we want to pick up that walkie talkie and get directions—"Come in, God. It's me." God doesn't communicate with us in quite that way—but he *does* communicate with us. He wants us to hear and follow His guidance as surely as we seek it.

So—where does that leave us? It leaves us trusting the goodness and constancy of God. We trust that He loves us. We trust that He hears us. We trust that our own insights, however sharp, can't be a substitute for the guidance He gives. When we hand our lives over to God— when we say, "God, I haven't heard you in a while, but I know that you're there, and I want to build my life around you"—we take those first, crucial steps onto the right path.

engage

Consider: What does the path ahead look like for you? Sometimes, God is working through our own instincts and reasoning to guide us—and we'll know that's the case when our instincts are consistent with the Word of God we have in the Bible. Are you growing in your trust of the Lord? Or are you relying *only* on your own instincts?

Week Nineteen: __/__/__
A Flashlight in the Dark

Again Jesus spoke to them, saying, "I am the light of the world. Whoever follows me will never walk in darkness but will have the light of life." – John 8:12

Jesus often used metaphors to help us understand things that are beyond our comprehension. He used pictures and stories of this world to help us understand things *beyond* this world.

Previously, we reflected on the "vine" metaphor, through which Jesus emphasized how important it is for us to stay *connected* to him. We can't receive the nutrients we need to grow as the people of Christ without staying intimately connected to Christ himself, like a leaf to a vine. Another metaphor Jesus commonly uses is that of light; the Gospels tell us that Christ *is* light. Just as God shattered pre-creation "nothingness" with a light He called into being, so did Christ dispel the darkness of a world disconnected from God. Remember how the wise men found Jesus after his birth? They navigated using the light of the stars overhead—small pinpoints of light piercing the otherwise dark sky overhead, showing the way to those who sought Jesus.

We might imagine Christ and his teachings like the light of a lantern we can cast over the path in front of us, helping us see the terrain before we make a misstep. We can choose well because of what Jesus' life and testimony illuminate for us; they show us how to be a part of something true, a part of something bigger—and they show us how to live.

engage

Consider: So far, we've reflected on a few gospel metaphors—including Christ as the vine and Christ as the light. Which do you like best? Why? How does that metaphor guide you in your relationship with Christ?

Week Twenty: __/__/__
Children of Light

Jesus said to them, "The light is with you for a little longer. Walk while you have the light, so that the darkness may not overtake you. If you walk in the darkness, you do not know where you are going. While you have the light, believe in the light, so that you may become children of light." After Jesus had said this, he departed and hid from them. – John 12:35-36

In the book of John, these are among Jesus' last words to his disciples. He was explaining to them that a time was coming when he wouldn't be with them—when they would have to abide in him in a different way. He wouldn't be able to answer their questions—however cryptically—in person.

Even after he explained this to the disciples, they didn't understand. How could they? The Son of God, in their imagining, wasn't someone who would die on a cross. They could not have prepared themselves for Jesus' death.

But we *can* understand, these many years later, because our whole lives have been lived without Jesus' physical presence. We're connected to Christ, as he promised we would be, by the Holy Spirit—but it's a different kind of relationship. When Jesus says, "the light is with you for a little while longer," we know what he means. When he left this world, and for the three days until his resurrection, it was as though someone had turned the lights out. By believing in Christ and soaking up all he said during his time among them, the disciples are still able to navigate in the darkness of his death.

engage

Consider: The moon doesn't actually emit any of its own light; it just reflects the light of the sun in the darkness! How can you be like the moon, reflecting the light of Christ even during the nighttime?

Week Twenty-One: __/__/__
Waiting on the Lord

For God alone my soul waits in silence;
from him comes my salvation.
He alone is my rock and my salvation,
my fortress; I shall never be shaken.
— Psalm 62:1-2

Have you heard that phrase before—"waiting on the Lord?" We usually say it when we want an answer; we want to know whether to turn right or left, whether to end a relationship or start something new. There's often an emphasis on the "waiting" because God makes things known in God's time. In an age of instant gratification—when queries can be resolved with a simple internet search or groceries ordered with the click of a button—it feels especially taxing to wait for God.

The Psalmist here is waiting on God to act and to speak. He wants revenge on those who persecute him; he wants God to accelerate God's justice—but he knows he must wait. How does he wait? In silence! Sometimes, God speaks loudly and clearly, like a thunderbolt, but sometimes, God speaks in a whisper. The psalmist waits in silence, in stillness, to make sure he can hear God when and however God speaks.

For the psalmist, God is worth waiting for. God brings salvation. God alone is unmoving, steady, and sure as a rock. It isn't easy to live in this place of total trust, but the psalmist tells us it's the only place his soul *can* rest. He's willing to stake his honor and his hope for his future on the dependability and goodness of God.

engage

Practice: Are you waiting on something in your life right now? To graduate, fall in love, get your own place? Maybe you've even prayed for God to take some action in your life—but you haven't felt God answer. This week, try this prayer:

God, sometimes, waiting is hard, and impatience gets the better of me. I can't see your bigger picture yet—and it discourages me. Help me to listen for your voice, even as you speak in unexpected ways. Help me to see your action all around me. You alone hold the future; help me to rest in confidence of your love and justice. Amen.

Week Twenty-Two: __/__/__
When We Feel Anxious

Do not be anxious about anything, but in every situation, by prayer and petition, with thanksgiving, present your requests to God. And the peace of God, which transcends all understanding, will guard your hearts and your minds in Christ Jesus.
— Philippians 4:6-7

Everyone, at some point, experiences anxiety. Most of the time, it's a totally normal response to stress. Imagine one of our ancestors running from a saber tooth tiger; she might have felt pretty anxious! In that kind of situation, anxiety was helpful. Stress hormones, when released in our bodies, help us better react to potentially dangerous situations.

Stress is less helpful when we're only *thinking* about a situation. We might anticipate a difficult test or a conversation we need to have with a friend or parent and begin to feel anxious. We might even feel anxious without being able to pinpoint why.

In his letter to the Church in Philippi, Paul recognizes aspect of our human experience. He encourages those in Philippi to lay their worries before God in prayer rather than feel anxiety about situations and outcomes beyond their control. We can't control the universe, Paul is saying, and we'll only stress ourselves out when we try to. We can't control what other people think about us anymore than we can control the texture of our hair. We can't control which colleges accept us, or which employers want to hire us. Anxiety will still surely crop up—it's a part of being human—but Paul encourages us to hand it over to God, letting our trust in God's love for us and purpose for our lives give us peace.

The truth is: God doesn't want us to feel anxious—but sometimes we will anyway. If it helps, you should consider talking to someone: a friend, a parent, or someone trained as a counselor.

engage

Practice: This week, when you're feeling anxious, try this prayer:

Listen, God, I'm feeling anxious. Please give me your peace—that otherworldly peace that surpasses all understanding. Blow this anxiety away like a storm cloud and bring serene skies for me. Amen.

Week Twenty-Three: __/__/__
In the Valley of the Shadow of Death

Even though I walk through the darkest valley, I will fear no evil, for you are with me; your rod and your staff, they comfort me. – Psalm 23:4

Do you know this psalm? Many, many people find special meaning in Psalm 23. One of the joys in praying this psalm and keeping it close to your heart, in fact, is knowing how many brothers and sisters in Christ find it deeply meaningful, too. It captures for many the comfort and companionship God offers us. Even when we're walking through a dim or unsettling part of our lives, we can be assured that God is with us.

The psalm begins with the famous line, "The Lord is my shepherd." We are led and watched over like beloved creature of a benevolent shepherd. He makes sure we are nourished and rested. He guides our steps so we stay on safe paths—but even when we venture away into danger, He pursues us and finds us. Do you remember Jesus' Parable of the Lost Sheep? Even with 99 sheep accounted for, God will search for and find the one lost sheep and bring her home.

That's a love that we can lean into, a love that envelops and holds us. No matter what you're going through—whether it's a relationship that feels broken beyond repair, a test you've failed, or even just sometimes feeling—God is there. God is with you, guiding you still.

engage

Go for it: This week, read Psalm 23 from your Bible and try to memorize it—maybe a few verses each day. The next time you're feeling discouraged or overwhelmed, try reciting whatever you remember of this psalm. How do the images of Psalm 23 comfort you?

Week Twenty-Four: __/__/__
No Need to Worry

"Therefore I tell you, do not worry about your life, what you will eat or drink; or about your body, what you will wear. Is not life more than food, and the body more than clothes?" – Matthew 6:25

Here's a passage I take to heart. I'm a planner; I make lists, and then I check things off. I think about tomorrow well before its arrival, and I worry about things that never do come to pass. Jesus urges his listeners here in Matthew to release this worry. They don't have to have everything figured out right now—they just have to follow him.

What's more, Jesus urges us to live a countercultural life; that is, a life that's not defined by pursuit of wealth and success. In our society, we always seem to want more *things*—and the more we have, the more we worry about losing it. In other words, in trying to buy our way to security, we make ourselves more and more anxious. Peace eludes us—even when we may feel we have everything else.

This doesn't mean we should care about whether *other* people have what they need—in fact, we *are* called to worry about whether our neighbor has food to eat or clothes to wear. We *are* called to worry about whether they are safe and secure. As biblical scholar Dale Bruner puts it, this passage isn't anti*social*; it's just anti*selfish*. Worrying about ourselves, especially when it orients us toward material things or comes at the expense of others, only drives a wedge between us and God. When we quit worrying about our*selves*—that's when the Spirit can really do amazing things in and through us.

engage

Consider: What are you worrying about that you might need to hand over to God in prayer this week? Is that worry getting in the way of your walk with Christ? How?

Week Twenty-Five: __/__/__
A Future with Hope

"For surely I know the plans I have for you," says the Lord, "plans for your welfare and not for harm, to give you a future with hope." – Jeremiah 29:11

In the sixth-century BC, the Jewish Kingdom of Judah fell to the Babylonian King Nebuchadnezzar and most of Jerusalem's residents were exiled to Babylon. Why the history lesson? This period of history played a significant role in shaping Jewish identity. Away from their ancestral homes, in a strange land, God's people struggled to understand how their fortunes had turned. They wondered when they would get to go home.

But, through the prophet Jeremiah, God told these people that they needed to hunker down and prepare to *stay*. In fact, he told them, their exile would last for generations—and most would not live to see their home again! Jeremiah encouraged them to build new homes, plant gardens, and pray for the welfare of the new city where they found themselves. His greatest encouragement was this: I have plans for you yet.

These plans, God promises the Israelites, are not for harm, not for despair or destruction. They're plans for your health, for your welfare. They are plans to *give you a future with hope*. Can you imagine hearing those words from a place of exile? How jolting they must have been to the hearer? Even when all seems lost, and we may even begin thinking that God has turned His back on us, we're reminded that God has plans for us yet—and these plans are *good*. We may not be able to predict how, but God can redeem even the darkest, worst experiences if we let Him. He'll give us a future with hope.

engage

Consider: Have you ever felt like you were in a place of exile? How have you seen God at work, even there?

Week Twenty-Six: __/__/__
Forgiveness without End

For you, O Lord, are good and forgiving, abounding in steadfast love to all who call on you. – Psalm 86:5

God created us, loves and cares for us—and we continually wander away. Over and over, God pursues us and brings us back like a lost lamb held gently in his arms. His forgiveness is everlasting. It never ends; we never exhaust it, no matter how many mistakes we make or how far we wander away from Him.

And forgiveness isn't easy. We know that from our own lives. When someone abandons us or rejects us, it hurts. We have trouble moving on, let alone forgiving. But God chooses to forgive us every time, because that's the kind of God He is. He's the kind of God who wants us back at all costs—even the cost of his Son on a cross. He's the kind of God that doesn't care where you've been as long as you're here. He's the kind of God before whom you can lay all your worries, all your sins, all your shortcomings—real or imagined. He's the kind of God who can handle all your doubt. He sees each of us at our most broken, and he wants us anyway.

God's forgiveness is inexhaustible because he loves us with a love that is pure, steady, and abiding. The healthiest relationships we experience in this world give us a foretaste of the love of God. His love is unconditional—there's not a single thing you must do to earn it or keep it. It's out of that love and that deep desire to be known by us that He forgives us again and again and again.

engage

Practice: Is there anything for which you need to seek God's forgiveness this week? Bring it before God in prayer. When we confess how we've moved away from God, we can trust that God will meet us with His incredible forgiveness.

Week Twenty-Seven: __/__/__
Lord, Teach Us to Pray

He was praying in a certain place, and after he had finished, one of his disciples said to him, "Lord, teach us to pray, as John taught his disciples." He said to them, "When you pray, say: Father, hallowed be your name. Your kingdom come. Give us each day our daily bread. And forgive us our sins, for we ourselves forgive everyone indebted to us. And do not bring us to the time of trial." – Luke 11:1-4

In the Gospel of Luke, one of the disciples witnesses Jesus praying and asks him: How should we pray? Jesus' response, also found in the Gospel of Matthew, has been prayed by Christians for the last two thousand years as the "Lord's Prayer." (Though very similar, the Lord's Prayer recorded in Matthew is a bit longer than Luke's version.)

Jesus didn't give us a long prayer—when we recite it together in worship, it takes us less than a minute—but it's beautifully comprehensive. When we pray the Lord's Prayer: We acknowledge the holiness of God and the truth of His reign. We anticipate the coming of the Kingdom of God—a reality where the vulnerable and powerless are exalted. We ask God for sustenance, forgiveness (including the ability to forgive others), and protection.

Jesus knew we'd sometimes struggle to find the right words to pray, so he gave us words that would cover everything. Jesus himself demonstrated the importance of prayer in his ministry. Over and over, the Gospels tell us he withdrew to a mountaintop or other quiet place to speak with God alone. Christ wanted us to have that same, intimate relationship with God—and he didn't want words to ever get in the way.

engage

Practice: This week, pray the Lord's Prayer (in its longer form from the gospel of Matthew, below) every day. What do you notice there that you may not have noticed before?

Lord's Prayer

Our Father, who art in heaven, hallowed be thy name. Thy kingdom come, thy will be done, on earth as it is in heaven. Give us this day our daily bread and forgive us our trespasses as we forgive those who trespass against us. Lead us not into temptation but deliver us from evil, for thine is the kingdom, the power, and the glory forever. Amen.

Week Twenty-Eight: __/__/__
Finding the Right Words

"When you are praying, do not heap up empty phrases as the Gentiles do; for they think that they will be heard because of their many words." – Matthew 6:7

Have you ever felt like you didn't have the *right words* to pray? Sometimes, especially in places where we typically pray aloud, we can suffer from 'performance anxiety' when it comes to prayer. You may wonder: Am I doing this right? Does my prayer sound as good as my neighbor's?

Jesus teaches here in Matthew that some prayers "sound good" but are empty. Their authors think because of their "many words" that they'll be heard—but the truth is that God doesn't care how poetic or intelligent our prayers sound. God cares what's on your heart when you pray. In fact, maybe God doesn't even "hear" the words at all—maybe he receives from you the truth behind them. He hears your *heart,* and all the gratitude, worry, and desire on it.

As followers of Christ, we are pray-ers. As Martin Luther put it, "To be Christian without prayer is no more possible than to be alive without breathing." So when you bring yourself honestly before God—wherever and however you are—you're "doing it right." The only wrong way to pray is to skip it altogether.

We were made to pray. We were made to be in ongoing dialogue with our loving Creator, lifting up all of our imperfections and anxieties that he might accept them from us and change them into something new—which is what God does best.

engage

Practice: Set aside some time each day—even just five or ten minutes—and pray to God the way you might talk to a close friend—no fancy words necessary. How does it feel—is that what your soul needed?

Week Twenty-Nine: __/__/__
Sighs too Deep for Words

Likewise the Spirit helps us in our weakness; for we do not know how to pray as we ought, but that very Spirit intercedes with sighs too deep for words.
– Romans 8:26

When Christ knew he was leaving his disciples, he promised to send the Holy Spirit, or "the Advocate," to be with us and guide us in the turbulent transition ahead. The Spirit, the Father, and the Son are the three "persons" of God—what we call the Trinity. Sometimes, we use other names to describe the Spirit, including "Holy Ghost," "Spirit of God," or even "the Comforter." Some people (like me!) even use the feminine pronoun "she" when referring to the Spirit. As believers, we interact with the Holy Spirit every day. The Spirit is the aspect of God that can dwell within each of us, joining us with the life and activity of God.

In prayer, the Holy Spirit plays a vital role: She puts words to those things which we cannot. Sometimes, we don't know what to say to God. Sometimes, our pain is just too deep—but the Holy Spirit can take those "sighs too deep for words" and pass them on to God. We can spend quiet time with God just *sighing*—and that's *prayer*. It's prayer because we're listening, because we're creating space and setting aside time to grow in awareness of God within and all around us.

Some scientific studies have shown that, when people are having or remembering a religious experience, there's a decrease in activity of the right parietal lobe—the self-oriented part of our brain. In other words, prayer helps us to access something beyond ourselves.

engage

Practice: Continue the prayer practice you began last week—and try to find some time to pray each day this week, even if it's just for a few minutes. (You can pray in the car, on the bus, on a jog!) How does praying make you *feel?* Does it help you connect to something beyond yourself?

Week Thirty: __/__/__
Prayers of Mary, Mother of Jesus

All these were constantly devoting themselves to prayer, together with certain women, including Mary the mother of Jesus, as well as his brothers." – Acts 1:14

In the Protestant tradition, Jesus' mother, Mary, sometimes gets lost in the shuffle. She had perhaps the most incredible life experience of any (fully) human being on earth: without having ever been with a man, she conceived a child—the Son of God—and delivered him in a manger. *Kings* visited her infant son to praise him. Then, when he reached adulthood, she had a front-row seat to his brief, powerful ministry. After Jesus had healed and taught for only a short period of time, he was nailed to a cross and left to die. According to the Gospel of John, when Jesus saw her standing near the cross where he hung, awaiting his death, crowned with thorns, he said, "[Dear] woman, behold your son!"

Mary, the mother of Jesus, watched her son grow up and then die a sudden, painful death. She also watched as Jesus' followers proclaimed the word of his resurrection and established the church of Jesus Christ. Within that early church, Mary stayed, and Mary *prayed*. She met her son in prayer.

The Book of Acts tells us much about the way prayer shaped the life of the early church. For early Christians, prayer was never a chore but a way to be with Christ. The same is true for us today: Prayer is a way to offer God the content of our whole hearts, so that our hearts might be transformed by God's love.

engage

Consider: Put yourself, for a moment, in Mary's shoes. Imagine *all* that she witnessed, all that she *endured*. What role would you play in the church of your son? What do you think Mary got out of prayer?

Week Thirty-One: __/__/__
Prayer that Transforms

Pray in the Spirit at all times in every prayer and supplication. To that end keep alert and always persevere in supplication for all the saints. —Ephesians 6:18

Corrie ten Boom, a Dutch Christian who helped many Jewish people escape the Nazi Holocaust by hiding them in her closet, once asked, "Is prayer your steering wheel or your spare tire?" What she meant, I think, was: Is prayer a last-resort effort? Do you pray when things are looking grim—and you're desperate for God's intervention? That's not a bad time to pray; it's a great time! It just isn't the *only* time to pray. Virtually every time is a great time to come before God in prayer—because prayer isn't so much about what's happening around us as it is what's happening *within* us.

Paul writes to the church in Ephesus that they should pray everything all the time—which is just to say that there's nothing we can't bring before God in prayer. Sometimes, we'll see our outward world change in a way that corresponds to what we've prayed; what we prayed *for* comes to pass. Other times, no matter how consistently or fervently we pray, we don't see the changes we'd like. We wonder, if we're honest, whether prayer really makes any difference at all.

Paul urges the Christians in Ephesus to pray all the time, about all things, because he has witnessed firsthand the most beautiful truth about prayer: that we labor in prayer not to deliver a changed world but a changed self—a heart renewed by focus on his present, a mind enlightened by His will. God's poetry is this: that He would bring forth the Kingdom of God not without us but among and through us, with the subtle act of prayer.

engage

Practice: Is there a prayer request to which you keep returning—something you deeply desire for yourself or in your life? Continue to pray for it this week, but pay close attention, too, to what the Spirit is doing within you as you pray. Are you feeling a shift in yourself or your prayer request?

Week Thirty-Two: __/__/__
Fishers of Men

As he walked by the Sea of Galilee, he saw two brothers, Simon, who is called Peter, and Andrew his brother, casting a net into the sea—for they were fishermen. And he said to them, "Follow me, and I will make you fish for people." Immediately they left their nets and followed him. – Matthew 4:18-20

Jesus lived among us to teach and preach multitudes, but he also drew a small group of men—and women!—close to him. He spent considerable, intimate time with them. The first two he called into relationship with him this way were Peter and Andrew, two brothers and fishermen. When Jesus found them, they were casting their nets into the sea—and Jesus made them an offer so enticing, they immediately dropped their nets and followed him. In an instant, their whole lives changed.

In this story, we don't learn much about Peter and Andrew or their motivations. The focus isn't on them; it's on the power of Jesus' invitation. Jesus asks them to become "fishers of men," drawing others to them like fish to a lure—only the 'lure' is the love of God that shines through them. He calls them to a life of meaning. They found the offer so compelling they dropped their nets immediately.

Not all of us are asked to leave behind our old lives when Christ calls us to a new one. Peter and James ceased to fish for, well, fish and became evangelists. Others might keep their same jobs, schools, and neighborhoods when they commit their lives to Christ—but suddenly, everything is given new meaning; everything becomes part of God's powerful, redemptive story.

That day, Jesus called out to two strangers: "Do you want to make something of your life—something that matters? Follow me!"

engage

Consider: When did you first truly feel called to new life in Christ? Was there anything you left behind? What did the new life look like for you?

Part Three:

To love your neighbor as yourself

Week Thirty-Three: __/__/__
Marked by Christ's Love

"I give you a new commandment, that you love one another. Just as I have loved you, you also should love one another. By this everyone will know that you are my disciples, if you have love for one another." – John 13:34-35

You may have heard the hymn, "They'll know we are Christians by our love." Those words were inspired by Jesus' words to his disciples on their last night together. Jesus urges them to remember him and his love by loving each other. Christ will no longer be among them; they will not have him to love them but must provide that same love to one another. As a community, they will be marked by this love. As the hymn says, others will *know* they are followers of Jesus Christ because they embody the same gentle lovingkindness that Christ did.

Of course, this isn't always the case. Some of us receive our deepest wounds within communities of faith. We don't *feel* Christ's love for us emanating from the other folks in the pews. In fact, we may feel only judgement and critique. This isn't how it's meant to be. Our human natures creep in and thwart our ability to demonstrate the love of Christ to one another in the real, enduring ways that Jesus was talking about.

Jesus was asking his disciples to care deeply about each other—and sometimes even to prioritize others' welfare above their own. He was asking them to encourage, sustain, invest in, and advocate for one another. He went on to warn the disciples that the world will misunderstand the disciples the way it misunderstood Jesus, but they will be able to withstand that adversity because of the love they share. They will draw others to their community because of that same love.

engage

Consider: How do others know you are a follower of Christ? Because you've told them? Would they know even before you shared because of the way you live?

Week Thirty-Four: __/__/__
Love One Another

God's love was revealed among us in this way: God sent his only son into the world so that we might live through him. In this love, not that we loved God but that he loved us and sent his Son to be the atoning sacrifice for our sins. Beloved, since God loves us so much, we also ought to love one another. – 1 John 4:9-11

God showed us how deeply He loved us by sending His son, Jesus, into the world. Jesus' life and death serve as a bridge between us and God; we're reunited as a family because of Jesus' act on the cross. God's sacrifice through Christ changed *everything* for us. It showed us, in the most powerful way imaginable, how much God loves us. God pursues each one of us, because the family isn't whole without us.

Because of that love we received and keep receiving—that *grace* that continues to pour out over us—we are meant to love one another. In fact, we were *made* for it. We were created and designed to be in relationship with each other, to care deeply about each other. Some people even think this is what is what the Bible means when it says we were made "in the image" of God! When we love people around us, we tap into the best part of ourselves. We let the Spirit of God work through us so that we may practice compassion and nurture just as God has compassion for and nurtures us. The story of Jesus' ministry serves as a guide for us as we navigate what kind of people to be in the world. Everywhere he went, Christ made people *whole*. He *loved* them. The Son of God, sent to live among us as an act of God's love, showed us love and care wherever he went.

engage

Practice: This week, try this prayer:

God of Love,

help me to share your love with everyone I meet today.

Help me to overcome my own preoccupation with what's going on in my own life—so I might be a conduit of your love in the world.

Help me to feel that love myself so I may share it naturally.

Amen.

Week Thirty-Five: __/__/__
The Bigger Picture

I have been crucified with Christ; and it is no longer I who live, but it is Christ who lives in me. And the life I now live in the flesh I live by faith in the Son of God, who loved me and gave himself for me. — Galatians 2:20

We are transformed when we make the change from thinking about ourselves to thinking about others. Having ambitions or desires isn't wrong, but it is fundamentally *self*-oriented. It keeps our attention and energy tightly focused on what's going on with us. We don't have a lot of bandwidth for everything—and everyone—else. We are our own first priorities.

Dedicating your life to Christ means widening the lens; we see, clearly, that we are not the center of the universe but a small, beloved piece within it. We still profoundly matter, as does what we do in and with our lives, but we "get" that we're part of a much larger whole.

This changes everything. We think less about what we "owe ourselves" and more about our deep responsibility to others. Part of our human nature is our desire to be "king" and matter more than everything else around us. Our physical bodies only exacerbate this—we feel our own hunger more profoundly than we can feel another's—but our hunger doesn't matter anymore than our neighbor's.

As Paul wrote in his letter to the Galatians, when we commit our lives to following Christ, we reject the lie that we are Everything. We become part of something so much bigger, and we are freed from the stress, discouragement, and fear of focusing on ourselves. That is *good news*.

engage

Go for it: Next time you're at a party or another social event, don't worry about saying or doing the right thing. Instead focus on shining the love and compassion of God on everyone you meet.

Week Thirty-Six: __/__/__
Holy Circle-Makers

"Blessed are the peacemakers, for they will be called children of God."
– Matthew 5:9

In the Beatitudes, a series of unsettling blessings in Jesus' Sermon on the Mount, Jesus explained that the Kingdom of God looks nothing like the earthly kingdoms we've come to know. Here on Earth, "success" looks like making lots of money, earning prestigious titles, or wielding power through leadership. We want to "get ahead" or "climb the ladder." In the Kingdom of God, on the other hand, success looks very different. Jesus tells us the last will be first and the first shall be last. Those who were rejected by this world, for being weak or vulnerable, for serving rather than ruling, will be *celebrated* by God.

Those who create peace in their communities, Christ tells us, will be called *children of God*. What greater distinction could you receive? Peacemakers make communities *whole*. They help build *circles* wherever they find themselves, circles that include everyone in true relationship. These aren't just people who themselves are considered "peaceful," though they almost certainly have a peace about them. These are people who *actively* create peace; they teach others how to be peaceful, too—they energetically and devotedly work for justice, for mercy, for healthy relationships in the whole community. They see themselves as part of a whole rather than prioritizing themselves above everything else—and that makes the whole community better.

engage

Consider: What circle of peace are you a part of? How are people made whole here? (Or: Is there a new circle of peace that you feel called to make?)

Week Thirty-Seven: __/__/__
Christianity 301

For the whole law is summed up in a single commandment, "You shall love your neighbor as yourself." – Galatians 5:14

Sometimes, it's hard to remember all the things we're supposed to do. Each of us plays many roles. We are a friend, a daughter, a girlfriend—and eventually, for some of us, a wife and mother, too. Even within our identity as followers of Christ, we can feel overwhelmed by all the things we think we are "supposed to do"—all the guidelines of behavior and lifestyle.

In this wonderful passage from Galatians, a letter Paul wrote to a group of people who were very concerned about rules, it gets boiled down to one thing: loving our neighbor. When we love our neighbors and consider their welfare alongside our own (easier said than done, I know), we're honoring the intention behind many other guidelines for living. When we love our neighbors, we practice humility—by not putting ourselves above other people but instead putting *other people* above us. When we love our neighbors, we share a glimpse of the unconditional, true love Christ has for us. When we love our neighbors, we let go of the other distractions and idols that distort our discipleship.

In other words, loving our neighbors as ourselves requires that we know first how to *love* at all, which Christ taught us. It also requires that we know how to love *ourselves* as part of God's wondrous creation. It's a little like testing into Advanced Spanish; when we demonstrate true, non-judgmental, whole-seeking Christian love for our neighbors, we're also demonstrating all the other things we know about God and His love.

engage

Go for it: This week, try standing up on behalf of someone else—a friend, a relative, or even a stranger. This isn't just about using your voice; this is about knowing this person's needs well enough to represent them.

Week Thirty-Eight: __/__/__
The Golden Rule

"In everything do to others as you would have them do to you; for this is the law and the prophets." – Matthew 7:12

You may have heard today's scripture before and never even realized it was from the Bible. In fact, it's something that Jesus taught us—to help us understand what it means to care for our neighbors. The folks who listened to Jesus in-person had just as hard a time understanding what it really meant to *love your neighbor* as we do today. It sounds simple—but it gets complicated and uncomfortable pretty quickly.

The Golden Rule is this: Treat people the way you'd like to be treated. We can't understand people's preferences perfectly (which makes a good argument for just *asking* them), but our own preferences can be a good proxy for theirs. For instance, if you wouldn't want a group of your friends to hang out without you, you probably shouldn't exclude one of your friends. If you wouldn't want someone to make fun of the way *you* dress, you probably shouldn't make fun of the way *she* dresses, *either.*

It isn't always simple. Sometimes, we'll still make mistakes. We'll do things that hurt other people and we'll depend on the grace of forgiveness to heal wounds between us. That's a part of life, and a part of human relationships. Nonetheless, it's a good rule of thumb to expect the things you'd find hurtful to be hurtful to other people, too. The reverse, too, is helpful: If something builds you up and gives you encouragement, you might try to offer the same thing to someone else. When in doubt, err on the side of caring too much—because, as Jesus taught, this is the way we really follow his example. His self-sacrificial, universal love will pave the way.

engage

Consider: Can you remember a time when you made a mistake in how you treated someone—maybe a friend or family member, or even a stranger—and caused him or her hurt? What did you learn about how to care for them?

Week Thirty-Nine: __/__/__
The Power of a Story

"Which of these three, do you think, was a neighbor to the man who fell into the hands of the robbers?" He said, "The one who showed him mercy." Jesus said to him, "Go and do likewise." – Luke 10:36-37

When Jesus thought those listening to him weren't quite "getting" it, he'd often tell a story. He knew just how powerful story is, and he wanted to give his followers concrete examples that spoke to their daily lives. We might wonder what sort of parables Jesus would tell us today—I like to imagine they'd incorporate Snapchat, texting, and politics.

The story of the Good Samaritan shows us what it looks like to "love our neighbor as ourselves." In the story, a Samaritan—a person from the neighboring but antagonistic kingdom of Samaria—is traveling on a dangerous path. Robbers and other criminals were known to lurk along this path, behind natural rock formations, preying on vulnerable travelers. One such traveler is beaten and left for dead. Jesus tells us that two other travelers—a priest and a Levite—walk right past the man. They see him, they understand he needs medical attention, but they decide not to be the ones to help. Then, along comes a Samaritan. A Samaritan wasn't a likely source of help; Jews and Samaritans had a long history of despising one another. The Samaritan had every reason to pretend, like the others, that he didn't see this man who so urgently needed help. But he didn't. He stopped. He showed the beaten traveler the compassion and care others had denied.

Jesus tells this story in response to the question "Who is my neighbor?" In the parable, the "neighbor" is the man who shows mercy to the beaten traveler—even though he had every excuse not to. He stepped in to help with all he had—his time, his money, even his own safety—for the sake of another, no matter what political party, ethnicity, or religion to which this other man belonged.

engage

Consider: Who is *your* neighbor? Think expansively! This story was meant to provoke its hearers to think about all new kinds of "neighbors" they might be called to help.

Week Forty: __/__/__
Entertaining Angels

Let mutual love continue. Do not neglect to show hospitality to strangers, for by doing that some have entertained angels without knowing it. – Hebrews 13:1-2

At our best, we're able to see in each other the preciousness of God's creation. We might look at someone—even someone who isn't being nice to us—and see the beauty of someone lovingly created and known by God. This is *hard*. But it's a challenge that Christians have to take on.

In the Bible, there are many stories of men and women "entertaining angels" without knowing it—Abraham, Lot, Gideon and others. Perhaps the most memorable of these moments was when Jesus traveled incognito on the Road to Emmaus with two other travelers. He didn't reveal himself to them; he just listened as they spoke about Jesus' death. Later, when they shared a meal together, he revealed himself—and they realized they'd been walking with Jesus all along.

The author of Hebrews is encouraging us, as people who want to be more like Christ, to *lavish* hospitality and love on those around us. We should try our best to treat the people who come into our lives like they're *royalty*—maybe even like they were Jesus himself. When we do this, we honor the one we follow, who would surely show them the same acceptance and love. Again—this isn't easy. Our commitment to this kind of caring is one we must renew again and again, trusting that the Spirit of God is with us every step of the way.

engage

Practice: This week, offer someone hospitality as though he or she were secretly royalty. (Just think: How would I act if I thought this person was really, really important?) What did that look like, and how did it feel?

Week Forty-One: __/__/__
Seeing the Value in Others

Do nothing from selfish ambition or conceit, but in humility regard others as better than yourselves. – Philippians 2:3

This week's verse comes from a letter Paul wrote to the Church in Philippi, a Roman colony on the coast of what is now Greece. Paul wrote this letter from a jail cell, where he had been imprisoned for preaching the Gospel. He urges his readers, then and now, to follow Jesus' example with their whole lives and to live with humility.

The word "humility" itself comes from the Latin word, *humilitas*, which can also mean "grounded" or "from the earth." When we practice humility as Christians, we acknowledge our created-ness. We recognize that we were shaped, lovingly, out of dust. We will never be the Creator but will always be the created; we don't try to make ourselves "king" over everyone else.

Jesus' life shows us what humility looks like. He was born in a manger to poor teenagers and died on a cross—neither worthy of a King. In between, during his lifetime, he never forcibly overthrew rulers to govern in their place or made peace with war. He did nothing with fanfare, never savored glory or fame. He taught, healed, and loved with simplicity and meekness.

We follow Christ's example when we stop prioritizing our own needs over our neighbors'. This isn't about our own worth—God sees us as valuable beyond compare—but about seeing ourselves as pieces of a much larger whole, every other piece of which is truly precious.

engage

Consider: Where do you feel "selfish ambition or conceit" in your life? Is there some skill, aptitude, or achievement that gives you particular pride? Has it ever gotten in the way of you regarding someone else as "better than you" the way Paul describes?

Week Forty-Two: __/__/__
A Word Against Judging Others

Let us therefore no longer pass judgment on one another, but resolve instead never to put a stumbling block or hindrance in the way of another. – Romans 14:13

Here, in Paul's Letter to the Romans, Paul was worried about division within the Christian community about how to live a Christian life. We still have these kinds of disagreements today, in just about every place where Christians gather. We want to live faithfully—but, sometimes, we all have different ideas about what this should look like.

Should women be ordained? Is homosexuality a sin? Is swearing "un-Christian"? Does a Christian have any special responsibility for caring about the environment? These are just a few of the questions modern churches grapple with—and these disagreements will likely continue for the foreseeable future.

Sometimes, these conversations are healthy and serve the greater unity of the church. At its best, sharing different views on an issue helps us clarify what we believe. Other times, focusing too much on disagreements can cause division and create cultures of judgement.

We're not meant to *judge* one another—that's God's job. We wouldn't be very good judges anyway; more than likely, some of the things we get worked up about mean less to God than things like caring for our neighbors. (I constantly find it a *relief* that I am *not* called to decide who is "in" or "out," who is "faithful" and who is a "hypocrite.) Our priority should instead be on helping people get closer to God, with love and humility.

engage

Practice: Ask God to help you manage the human tendency to judge other people around you with this prayer:

God, I can't help but judge people around me who don't seem to live their lives from a place of rootedness in you and your word. I know it's not my job, but sometimes, I can't help it. Please free me from this habit so I might see the goodness in people—as You see the goodness in each of your creatures—and leave any judgment to you. Help me to be preoccupied only with showing your love and helping others grow in love of you.

Week Forty-Three: __/__/__
That God's Works Might be Revealed

As he walked along, he saw a man blind from birth. His disciples asked him, "Rabbi, who sinned, this man or his parents, that he was born blind?" Jesus answered, "Neither this man nor his parents sinned; he was born blind so that God's works might be revealed in him." – John 9:1-3

In this story from the Gospel of John, Jesus and the disciples encounter a blind man—and the disciples want to know *why*. They actually give Jesus two options: either this man had sinned, or his parents had. They assume there is a cause-and-effect relationship between this man's blindness and some offense against God. Otherwise, how could this bad thing have happened?

When bad things happen to each of us, we may wonder if we're being punished. Some losses we experience in life are so great that it is hard to reconcile them with a God who loves and cares for us. Maybe, like the man who was blind, we can identify some aspect of our body or being that isn't the way we would wish it to be. Asking God "why?"— as the Psalms demonstrate in abundance—is definitely fair game.

But Jesus' reply to the disciples gets to the heart of something: What we suffer in life isn't the consequence of something we've done wrong, or even necessarily something God "does" to us. We live in a world that is broken—that we all have helped, in our own ways, to break— and there is real suffering here. Jesus' reply corrects the disciples' own flawed sight: This man isn't blind because of sin—but God can still work through the man's blindness. God can redeem even the worst experiences. For the blind man in Jesus' path that day, this literally meant enabling him to see—helping him to pass from darkness to light.

engage

Consider this: Is there something bad that has happened to you that you've felt God at work through? How?

Week Forty-Four: __/__/__
The New Commandment

"I give you a new commandment, that you love one another. Just as I have loved you, you also should love one another." – John 13:34

In the Old Testament, many years before the birth of Jesus, Moses climbed to the top of Mt. Sinai, where God gave him ten laws to share with the people of Israel—the "Ten Commandments." The people of God fell short of these laws repeatedly, but the Ten Commandments offered guidance for centuries.

In his time among us on earth, Jesus said that he came not to overturn the law but to "fulfill it"—that is, to show people how to truly live a Godly life. As human beings, we do our best to interpret and live according to God's will, but it's incredibly challenging. We may disagree about what God's will really is. That uncertainty and disagreement is what Jesus spoke to with his ministry.

As he neared the end of his time with his disciples, Jesus gave them this new commandment—and asked them to show the same kind of love to one another that he showed them. There is no greater love than the love Christ showed us—literally sacrificing his life on our behalf. With these words, Jesus seems to be acknowledging that disagreement and disunity will continue to crop up; it's part of our human natures, even in communities of faith. What will restore health is this: remembering that loving one another *as Jesus loved us* is above everything else.

engage

Consider: Do you ever get caught up in the "rules" of Christian living? Are the rules truly helping you to become more like Christ—or are they getting in the way? Do you honor Christ's "new commandment" of loving everyone around you as he loved the disciples?

Week Forty-Five: __/__/__
A Vessel of God's Love

And may the Lord make you increase and abound in love for one another and for all, just as we abound in love for you. – 1 Thessalonians 3:12

If you have been trying to practice love of neighbor lately, you know: it's tough stuff. We are called to love and care for our neighbors in ways that are stretching, challenging—and meaningful. We're not always reaching out to the people we feel most comfortable with, or even those easiest to love.

What Paul writes to the community in Thessalonica here is more a prayer than instruction. To be sure, Paul hopes that Christians will show radical love to one another—but he knows that love comes from somewhere beyond us. Our prayer, consistently, is that God would pour God's love into us so abundantly that it would overflow and spill on everyone around us. It's a nice image, isn't it? We're the vessels of God's love, and all we have to do is *receive* for everyone to be blessed.

That's *good news*. Loving our neighbors isn't all up to us! (Hallelujah!) If we tried to follow Christ's example and love our neighbors without drawing from the well of Christ within us, we'd run dry quickly. We'd fall well short of Christ's example. But God loves every part of his creation, from the nightshade berry to the blue whale—and everything (and one!) in between. His love is genuine, unconditional, and inexhaustible. When we're receiving God's love and letting it splash onto our neighbors, we're giving them something far greater than what might have come directly from us. What's more, as Paul hints here in this letter, the more Christ is at work within us, the more that love of our neighbor grows.

engage

Consider: What helps you to *receive* God's love? (When do you *feel* loved by God most deeply?) Is it meditating on His word, meeting Him in regular prayer, experiencing the wonder of his creation—or even all the above?

Week Forty-Six: __/__/__
Radical Hospitality

Welcome one another, therefore, just as Christ has welcomed you, for the glory of God. – Romans 15:7

God wants us to welcome and accept one another—to "reach out and welcome one another to God's glory!" as American pastor and writer Eugene Peterson phrased it. You may have heard people talk about "radical Christian hospitality," which isn't just about inviting people into your home. Hospitality means meeting people where they are at in their lives and drawing them in with love. It really can be that simple.

Our inspiration, of course, is Christ himself—who reached beyond every human boundary (gender, ethnicity, nationality) to accept and love those whose paths crossed his. With Jesus, there were no "insiders" and "outsiders," no "cool" group or "losers." Everyone received the same warm embrace, the same care and compassion. Even Pontius Pilate, who played a vital role in Jesus's death, could have been in community with Christ if he'd opened his heart to God's message. Jesus didn't *agree* with everyone—but he didn't exclude anyone from his ministry.

"Welcome" is a powerful thing. Where human brokenness may inspire us to build walls and boundaries, our identity in Christ calls us to tear down those walls and transgress those boundaries. When we welcome people into our lives the way that Christ welcomed us, we begin to create the kind of unity and harmony that makes God's love feel real to people in our community.

How awesome would it be if people in your life saw you as someone of acceptance and universal care? What if your friends—and even people you don't know that well—knew they would feel special when they hung out with you? *That's* the radical hospitality to which we're called.

engage

Go for it: This week, offer someone the acceptance and love of Christ—maybe someone who has been in your life for a while, or someone you're just getting to know. As you approach your time together, think, "How can I make this person feel loved and cared for today?"

Week Forty-Seven: __/__/__
Mercy in the World

"Be merciful, just as your Father is merciful." – Luke 6:36

What does it mean to be "merciful"? We think of mercy most often in life-or-death situations—in an ancient Roman coliseum, the emperor might have "shown mercy" by sparing the life of a defeated gladiator, for example. It's unlikely you're going to be in a position to spare someone's *life*—so what could this instruction mean to you?

These words come from Jesus, in his Sermon on the Plain in the Gospel of Luke. (The Sermon the Plain is Luke's version of Matthew's longer "Sermon on the Mount," a collection of Jesus' teachings, including the Beatitudes.) Jesus had been talking about loving our enemies, and even "turning the other cheek" as a way to responding to injury without revenge. As if his listeners might have trouble motivating themselves to offer this kind of peacefulness in the face of others' ill-intent, Jesus reminds them: *God* is merciful. We ought to show those around us compassion and mercy because *God* has shown each of you an abundance of mercy through Christ. Our journey as Christians is to become more "Christlike" in our words and deeds—a process called "sanctification." Mercy is a big piece of that puzzle.

The world encourages us to hold grudges and keep running lists of the hurt we receive at the hands of others. We might even dream of or pursue revenge—or maybe simple harden our hearts and resolve never to show vulnerability again. What Jesus teaches here is that mercy is the way of the kingdom. Vulnerability and compassion are not weakness—as the world would have us believe—but true strength.

engage

Consider: We show "mercy" rather than just "forgiveness" when we hold more power than the person who has hurt us. You might not even appreciate the power you have in some relationships—because it might be slight, or highly informal. Where do you have or exercise power that you may not have appreciated?

Week Forty-Eight: __/__/__
Peace on Earth

For a child has been born for us, a son given to us; authority rests upon his shoulders; and he is named Wonderful Counselor, Mighty God, Everlasting Father, Prince of Peace. – Isaiah 9:6

Even hundreds of years before Christ's birth, he was expected and eagerly anticipated. Isaiah had prophesied about a child who would enter the world and be called all these special names: "Wonderful Counselor, Mighty God, Everlasting Father, and Prince of Peace." Many still understand this prophecy to be about Jesus Christ.

At the time of Jesus' birth, "peace" meant something specific: the absence of war. In fact, Jesus entered the world during the *Pax Romana*, a long period of relative peace and stability established through the might of the Roman Empire. During this period, the empire had expanded to the point that nearly a third of the world's population was under Roman rule. That, for Jesus' contemporaries, was *peace*. Augustus, the emperor on whom this peace dawned, was considered a Peacemaker. Imagine a modern example: If your city council put every dissenter on its payroll, would that be peace? Imagine if, after an argument between a sibling, your mother enforces a "no talking" rule. Is that peace?

Jesus brought a new peace—one that included justice, mercy, equity, and love. The difference between the world's peace and Christ's peace is like the difference between solid wood and a thin veneer; the world's peace seems thin and cheap by comparison.

engage

Go for it: Try to bring Christ's peace to bear on a relationship where you might just have worldly peace. Is there a friendship where you've agreed to "not be friends"? Can you bring true peace to it?

Week Forty-Nine: __/__/__
The Healing Power of Forgiveness

Then Peter came and said to him, "Lord, if another member of the church sins against me, how often should I forgive? As many as seven times?" Jesus said to him, "Not seven times, but, I tell you, seventy-seven times."
– Matthew 18:21-22

Forgiving others for the harm they do to us can be among the most challenging things we do. It's not terribly difficult to forgive someone for bumping into us in the hallway, or maybe even for genuinely forgetting to invite us to a party. We might feel hurt for a few days, but eventually, we're ready to offer forgiveness and mend the relationship.

There are other harms done to us in this world that are much greater, and we might spend years or even most of our lifetime trying to forgive. When Peter asked Jesus how often he should forgive— expecting a specific, low number ("seven times")—Jesus turns his idea on its head. "Seventy-seven times!" Jesus answers. Of course, Jesus didn't mean we should keep a running list of the forgiveness we offer someone else; he meant for us to forgive the seventy-*eighth* time, too.

Jesus wishes for us to forgive because it's good for community but, more importantly, because it's good *for us*. There's an unattributed quote: "Holding on to anger is like drinking poison and expecting the other person to die." When we withhold forgiveness and continue to nurture our anger or indignation, we pollute our souls. We choke out the love and grace that Christ is working to bring into the world through us.

engage

Consider: Is there anyone from whom you're withholding forgiveness? How has that affected YOU?

Week Fifty: __/__/__
Forgiving Others as God Forgives Us

"For if you forgive others their trespasses, your heavenly Father will also forgive you; but if you do not forgive others, neither will your Father forgive your trespasses."
– Matthew 6:14-15

When Jesus taught the disciples how to pray what we now call "The Lord's Prayer," he concluded with these words. Others' "trespasses" (an old legal term) are things they've done to offend, hurt, or do wrong against us. The point isn't that God only forgives us according to our capacity for forgiveness—but that God's forgiveness should *inspire* our own.

God loves us—each of us—so much that he gave up his son so that we might be forgiven our brokenness and forever reconciled to him. That's an incredible love, and forgiveness that we did nothing to earn. When we pray to God that he might forgive us for something that we've done, some way that we've fallen short of his plans for us in our daily life, we should also be praying that we would be able to forgive others for whatever they've done to offend us. We can't ask God for forgiveness while simultaneously hardening our hearts toward others.

Prayer is the place where God works most deeply on our hearts, bringing us into closer alignment with His will and His ways. This is, perhaps, why Jesus makes these remarks just after giving the disciples The Lord's Prayer. In prayer, as we ask God to make us whole again, we aspire to be able to offer some of that wholeness to others through forgiveness. Sometimes, this forgiveness will happen gradually, over a long period of time; often, we cannot forgive as easily as we can say the words "I forgive you." That's all right—it's still a very worthwhile undertaking.

engage

Practice: This week, ask God to work on your power to forgive. It may be a long journey—especially if the harm you wish to forgive is significant—but God can handle that long journey. Ask:

God, you know my heart better than I do; there's no part of it hidden from You. Help me to cleanse my heart of the grudges and hurt that it keeps holding onto. As You've forgiven me so frequently and completely, help me to work on forgiving others.

Week Fifty-One: __/__/__
To Be a Servant

"So if I, your Lord and Teacher, have washed your feet, you also ought to wash one another's feet." – John 13:14

In the time of Jesus, it was ordinary for hosts to offer guests water to wash their own feet, especially after a long journey in sandals on a dusty road. A household slave or servant would often be assigned the task. Other times, disciples might even wash their teacher's feet.

On the night before his death, Jesus, the teacher and master, washed his disciples' feet. One disciple, Peter, protested; it defied his expectations of a teacher-disciple relationship. Jesus was also beginning to act funny around them, as though the end were near, and this made them distraught. Finally, Peter allowed Jesus to wash his feet, and the rest followed.

Jesus washed the disciples' feet to show them, concretely, by personal example, what it meant to lead others through loving humility. He turned social standards on their head. Custom dictated that Jesus have the disciples wash *his* feet—but Jesus was teaching the disciples that the way of Christ is the way of servanthood. True leaders in Christ are those who humble themselves in service to others—those who seek out the unpopular; speak up for the minority viewpoint, even if it isn't their own, so it may be heard; and clean up—literally and figuratively— messes not of their own making. This is deeply subversive in a society where many of us fear being "taken advantage of." We don't want to seem like a "chump," someone easily manipulated for others' purposes. To be like Jesus, though, we do have to risk being taken advantage of—that's what Christlike vulnerability requires. Remember, on the night Jesus washed the disciples' feet, he even washed the feet of Judas—the man who would betray Jesus to his death. *That* is how committed Christ was to servanthood.

engage

Consider: In what ways do you follow Christ's example of servanthood with your life? Can you think of new ways of serving others to which God might be calling you?

Week Fifty-Two: __/__/__
Living for More

And [Mary] gave birth to her firstborn son and wrapped him in bands of cloth, and laid him in a manger, because there was no place for them in the inn.
— Matthew 2:7

The birth of Jesus Christ was not regal but understated, even humble. Mary and Joseph had made a journey back to their place of residence to be registered for the Roman census. Mary delivered baby Jesus in modest lodging, and after swaddling him, she laid him in an animal feedbox, or manger.

God's beloved son, who would live to teach us and die to save us from the consequences of our own sin, wasn't born like a king. This is the "scandal" of Christ, and of the cross itself. God didn't use grandiose means to display His power; he used a pink-cheeked, vulnerable human baby born to poor teenagers. Jesus didn't forcibly overthrow earthly rulers and govern in their place, making peace with war; he ultimately let them put him to death on a cross like a criminal.

This is the God we worship—a God of radical peace and unconditional love, whose ways are not our ways, and who passionately pursues each of us. Through the Holy Spirit, He works through our hearts not that we might be forced into submission, but that we might be inspired to live a life defined by His love.

This love, when it really catches us, transforms us into new creations. The old life falls away and a new life begins—a life rooted in the abundance and benevolence of Christ. We no longer live for ourselves or the flimsy tokens of this world but for something much, much bigger.

engage

Go for it: Write a letter to your future self, one you can set aside and read a year from now. What would you say? What would you hope for yourself? Your relationships? Your walk with God?

Epilogue

If you've been reading one entry about every week, it's been a year since you first held *Simple Truths* in your hand. You've been reflecting on God's word and journaling your response—even if intermittently—for a year. I hope it feels like a meaningful achievement.

Life and faith are dynamic—we may think, at times, that we have "figured it all out" or have it "mastered," but the truth is, we're always pilgrims searching for God. Even the wisest and most faithful adults in your life have places where they experience doubt or uncertainty. This doesn't make them less wise or less faithful; it only makes them fully human.

We worship a God who understands our humanity—and literally met us within it. I believe He doesn't want us to become "experts" of our faith so much as He wants us to be humble, earnest *learners* of it. I believe He wants you to seek Him and His will, however imperfectly, all your life. There's no friend or relative whose love is so steadfast and unconditional. Scripture tells us—*promises* us—that nothing can separate you from Him. You can put that in your pocket and pull it out when you need it, because that's an eternal truth, too.

Thank you for letting me be a part of your journey.

About the Author

Therin Jones Fenner is a Presbyterian pastor, writer, speaker, and mother of two. She received a BA from Stanford University and an MDiv from Princeton Theological Seminary. She currently works with Renewal Ministries Northwest, a Seattle-based Christian nonprofit that helps people listen to God through prayer retreats, spiritual direction, and other spiritual discernment. She's enthusiastic about running, Japanese food, and new expressions of Christ's church.